MW00718643

Feel the Spirit

Thirty-five Arrangements for Mixed Chorus
By MOSES HOGAN
With a Foreword by André Thomas

ISBN 978-0-634-05844-8

HAL•LEONARD®
CORPORATION
7777 W. BLUEMOUND RD. P.O. BOX 13819 MILWAUKEE, WI 53213

Copyright © 2003 by HAL LEONARD CORPORATION
International Copyright Secured   All Rights Reserved

No part of this book shall be reproduced or transmitted in any form or by any means,
electronic or mechanical, including photocopying, or by any information
storage or retrieval system without permission from the publisher.

Printed in the United States of America

Send all inquiries to:
Hal Leonard Corporation
7777 W. Bluemound Rd.
Milwaukee, WI 53213

Feel the Spirit

CONTENTS

FOREWORD

"For they that carried us away captive required of us a song;
and they that wasted us required of us mirth, saying, Sing
us one of the songs of Zion. How shall we sing the Lord's song
in a strange land?" Psalm 137:3-4

In 1619, the first Africans arrived in the English Colonies at Jamestown, Virginia. Thus began slavery in what was to become The United States of America. Alice Parker states, in her liner notes for the 1958 Robert Shaw Chorale recording of *Deep River and Other Spirituals*, "Why it is that 'man's inhumanity to man' should often produce great art is one of the mysteries of the human spirit." Yes, indeed a mystery, but these strong people did indeed create perhaps one of the greatest Art forms in America, the Negro Spiritual.

Although initially utilized in both slave worship and all other aspects of slave life on rural plantations in the South, the spiritual is a song that grew quickly in recognition and stature. Eventually, a group of young black singers would bring this song to the attention of the world. These young singers were students at Fisk University. Initially, they embarked upon a tour to raise money to help with the building program at their university. Little did they realize the immense effect of their efforts in the popularization of these songs. With the success of this ensemble, many other groups emerged in imitation of this ensemble. According to Eileen Southern (author of *The Music of Black Americans*), "by the end of the nineteenth century there were few places in the world that had not heard black America's spirituals and plantation songs."

By the nineteen twenties, black composers began to emerge and other special choral ensembles came into existence. Both the choral ensembles and the composers were indeed interested in the performance or arrangements of these songs. In February of 1928, the Hall Johnson Choir made its formal debut. By this time, Eva Jessye was active with her choir, the Original Dixie Jubilee Singers, and then the Eva Jessye Choir. In 1930, appointed musical director for the Broadway production of *Green Pastures*, Hall Johnson led the choir in singing spiritual arrangements for this play. In 1936, this play was made into a movie. Likewise, Eva Jessye wrote and arranged music for her choirs. In 1931, she wrote *The Life of Christ in Negro Spirituals*. She was such an influence on this music that Composer Virgil Thomson wanted her as choral director for *Four Saints in Three Acts*, and in 1935, George Gershwin wanted her for his production of *Porgy and Bess*.

The nineteen twenties also birthed the growth of the Negro College choirs—particularly the choirs of R. Nathaniel Dett, at the Hampton Institute, and William Dawson, music director at Tuskegee Institute. Both choirs toured and performed arrangements by their conductors. Other black institutions produced touring groups with Howard University, Morehouse College, included with many others. It was the arrangements by the conductors of these choirs, as well as others, which established what choral musicians today consider the traditional settings of these songs.

Moses Hogan has been a faithful steward of the traditional settings of these slave songs. It is easy to see the influence of William Dawson, Jester Hairston, Nathaniel Dett, John Work, and others in these highly crafted settings of these songs. Although steeped in tradition, Mr. Hogan breathes new life, harmonically and compositionally, into his settings. Harry T. Burleigh (who published the first arrangements of spirituals for solo voice) wrote of his personal aim, "My desire was to preserve them (the spirituals) in harmonies that belong to modern methods of tonal progression without robbing the melodies of their racial flavor." (New York World, October 25, 1924) Like Mr. Burleigh, Moses Hogan has the unique ability to expand harmonic considerations and maintain the racial flavor and tradition of settings. Like many of his predecessors, he has honed his arrangements, by having them performed by his own ensemble, The *Moses Hogan Chorale*, and later the *Moses Hogan Singers*. The arrangements have now found their home in the repertoire of choral ensembles throughout the entire world. These arrangements are heard at the state, divisional, and national conventions of the American Choral Directors Association, Music Educators National Conference, The World Symposium of the International Federation of Choral Musicians, and the National Association of Negro Musicians.

Perhaps no other arranger, in the past ten years, has been so influential in the revitalization of the songs of our forefathers. I am confident that those great arrangers of the past would look with pride on the quality and craftsmanship of these arrangements. Perhaps even more importantly, these distinguished arrangements reflect the dignity of a strong and proud people. As you sing these arrangements you will sense the unconquerable spirit and as Alice Parker states: "…(spirituals) have formed a language which leaps over national and racial boundaries, speaking to all men in uniquely rich and varied art."

Enjoy,

André Thomas
Friend of Moses Hogan

ANDRÉ J. THOMAS, the Owen F. Sellers Professor of Music, is Director of Choral Activities and Professor of Choral Music Education at Florida State University. He is frequently in demand as a choral adjudicator, clinician, and director of Honor Choirs and All-State Choirs throughout the United States, Europe, Asia, New Zealand and Australia. From 1993 to 1995, he served as President of the Florida American Choral Directors Association. In 2002, he became President of the Southern Division of the American Choral Directors Association.

MOSES GEORGE HOGAN, born in New Orleans, Louisiana on March 13, 1957, has received acclaim as a pianist, conductor and arranger of international renown. A graduate of the New Orleans Center for Creative Arts (NOCCA) and Oberlin Conservatory of Music in Ohio, he also studied at New York's Juilliard School of Music and Louisiana State University in Baton Rouge. Mr. Hogan's many accomplishments include winning first place in the prestigious 28th annual Kosciuszko Foundation Chopin Competition in New York and his appointment as Artist In Residence at Loyola University in New Orleans. Hogan began his exploration of the choral music idiom in 1980 leading to his founding of the New Orleans-based and internationally acclaimed *Moses Hogan Chorale*.

The *Moses Hogan Singers* made their debut in 1998 on the EMI record label with soprano Barbara Hendricks. Hogan was commissioned to arrange and perform several compositions for the 1995 PBS Documentary, THE AMERICAN PROMISE, whose soundtrack was released separately by Windham Hill records under the title *Voices*.

In addition, his discography includes *An American Heritage of Spirituals*, sung by the famed Mormon Tabernacle Choir, conducted by Moses Hogan and Albert McNeil; two recordings of spirituals with renowned countertenor Derek Lee Ragin on Aria Records and on Channel Classic Records; *This Little Light of Mine*, featuring Hogan's most recent commissions and dedications, with excerpts from the "Oxford Book of Spirituals," MGH Records; *The Moses Hogan Choral Series 2002*, features a collection of thirty-nine spirituals and songs of faith, sung by the *Moses Hogan Chorale* and *Moses Hogan Singers*, with excerpts from the "Oxford Book of Spirituals," produced and arranged by Moses Hogan, MGH Records; *Lift Every Voice For Freedom*, a collection of American folk songs, poems, hymns, songs of faith and patriotic songs.

Hogan served as editor of the new "Oxford Book of Spirituals," an expansive collection of spirituals, published by Oxford University Press. Hogan's contemporary settings of spirituals, original compositions and other works have been revered by audiences and praised by critics including Gramophone magazine. With over 70 published works, Hogan's arrangements have become staples in the repertoires of high school, college, church, community and professional choirs worldwide. Hogan's choral style, high musical standards and unique repertoire have consistently elicited praise from critics worldwide.

Dedicated to Professor Joseph Schwartz
Oberlin Conservatory of Music
Sung by The Oberlin College Choir, Hugh Floyd, Director

Abide with Me

For SATB div. a cappella

Performance Time: Approx. 3:30

Arranged by
MOSES HOGAN

Words by HENRY F. LYTE, 1847
Music by WILLIAM H. MONK, 1861

Copyright © 1999 by HAL LEONARD CORPORATION
International Copyright Secured   All Rights Reserved

Help of the help-less, O a - bide with me.

Help of the help-less, O a - bide with me.

Help of the help-less, O a - bide with me.

Help of the help-less, O a - bide with me.

I need Thy pres - ence ev - 'ry pass - ing hour.

I need Thy pres - ense ev - 'ry pass - ing hour.

I need Thy pres - ense ev - 'ry pass - ing hour.

I need Thy pres - ence ev - 'ry pass - ing hour.

14

15

* Close N of each a-me(n) to hum through ending.

Ain't That Good News

For SATB a cappella

Perfomance Time: Approx. 1:50

Arranged by
MOSES HOGAN

Traditional Spiritual

Copyright © 1997 by HAL LEONARD CORPORATION
International Copyright Secured   All Rights Reserved

I got a robe up in___ a that king-dom, ain't a that good news.___

good news.___ Good news,___ good news,___ good news,___ got

I'm a gon-na lay down___ this world,_____ gon-na should-er up___ a my

good news. Got good news,___ good news,___ good news,___

world,_____ gon - na should - er up__ a my cross,_____ gon - na take it home_ a to my

good news,_____ good news,_____ good news, good news,

Je - sus, ain't a that good news. I got a

good news, got news. Hm____

news.____ I got news,___ I got news, O Lord,_ I got good news.__

lay down_ this world,_____ gon - na should - er up_ a my cross,____ gon - na

good news,_ good news,__ good news,_ good news,_

sing my song_ a for my Je - sus,_ I'm gon - na play my harp_ a for my Je - sus,_ I'm gon - na

good news, good news,_ good news, good news,_

The Battle of Jericho

For SATB a cappella

Performance Time: Approx. 2:15

Arranged by
MOSES HOGAN

Traditional Spiritual

Copyright © 1996 by HAL LEONARD CORPORATION
International Copyright Secured   All Rights Reserved

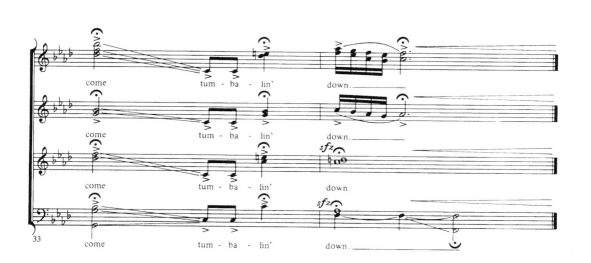

Didn't My Lord Deliver Daniel?

For SATB div. a cappella

Performance Time: Approx. 2:40

**Arranged by
MOSES HOGAN**

Traditional Spiritual

Copyright © 1999 by HAL LEONARD CORPORATION
International Copyright Secured   All Rights Reserved

To my parents,
Mr. Moses Hogan and Mrs. Gloria Hogan

Do Lord, Remember Me

For SATB div. a cappella

Performance Time: Approx. 3:25

Traditional Spiritual
Arranged by MOSES HOGAN

Copyright © 2001 by HAL LEONARD CORPORATION
International Copyright Secured   All Rights Reserved

45

46

Dedicated to the 1998 Ohio-Michigan Choral Festival
at St. Joseph's Church in Sylvania, Ohio
with Bedford H.S., Mark Smith; Northview H.S., Ben Ayling;
and Otsego H.S., Janine Baughman

Down by the Riverside

For SATB a cappella
Performance Time: Approx. 2:25

Arranged by
MOSES HOGAN

Traditional Spiritual

Copyright © 1999 by HAL LEONARD CORPORATION
International Copyright Secured   All Rights Reserved

50

war no more, war no more.__ I ain't gon-na stud-y war no more,__

14

__ ain't gon-na stud-y war no more,__ ain't gon-na stud-y war no

18

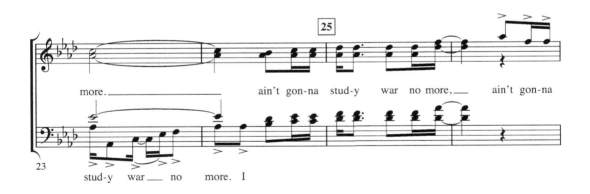

more._____ ain't gon-na stud-y war no more,__ ain't gon-na

stud-y war__ no more. I

23

stud-y war no more,__ ain't gon-na stud-y____ war no

27

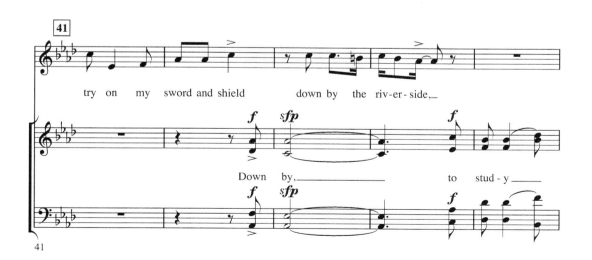

war no more, war no more.___ I ain't gon-na stud-y war no more,___

___ ain't gon-na stud-y war no more,___ ain't gon-na stud - y war no

more._____ ain't gon-na stud-y war no more,___ ain't gon-na

stud-y war___ no more. I

stud-y war no more,___ ain't gon-na stud - y_____ war no

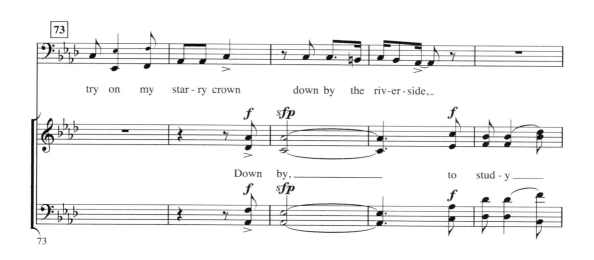

war no more, war no more.___ I ain't gon-na stud-y war no more,___

___ ain't gon-na stud-y war no more,___ ain't gon-na stud - y war no

more._____ ain't gon-na stud-y war no more,___ ain't gon-na

stud-y war___ no more. I

stud-y war no more,___ ain't gon-na stud - y_____ war no more.

Elijah Rock

For SATB (divisi) a cappella

Performance Time: Approx. 3:05

Traditional Spiritual

Arranged by
MOSES G. HOGAN

Copyright © 1994 by HAL LEONARD CORPORATION
International Copyright Secured   All Rights Reserved

56

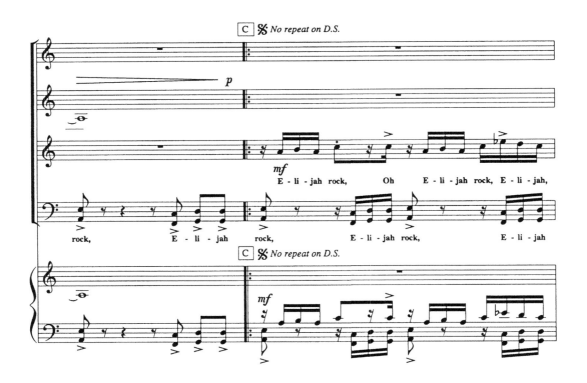

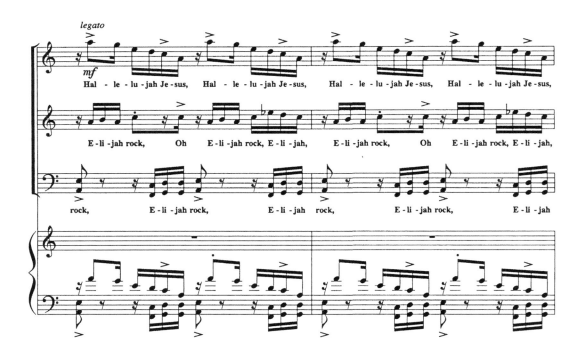

All Parts - Close to ending consonants on "Com", "In" and "I'm".

As Sung by DEREK LEE RAGIN
and THE MOSES HOGAN CHORALE

Ev'ry Time I Feel The Spirit

For SATB a cappella
Performance Time: Approx. 2:20

Traditional Spiritual

Arranged by
MOSES HOGAN

Copyright © 1995 by HAL LEONARD CORPORATION
International Copyright Secured   All Rights Reserved

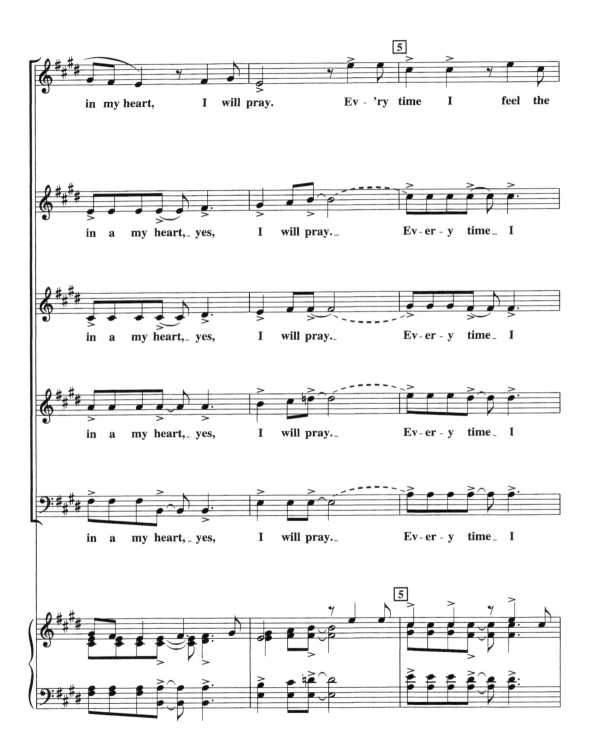

mouth came   fire   and smoke.   Down in the   val - ley,   on   my
bod - y   not   the soul.   All   a - round me   looked   so
heav - en   and   right back.   St. Pe - ter   wait - in'   at the

ooh.   Ooh, ___

ooh.   Ooh, ___

ooh.   Ooh, ___

ooh.   Ooh, ___

poco a poco dim.

div.

70

D.S.
(3rd time no repeat)

knees, asked my Lord have mer - cy please. Ev - 'ry
fine, asked my Lord if all was mine. Ev - 'ry
gate, said come on sin - ner, don't be late. Ev - 'ry

ooh. _____ Ev - 'ry

ooh. _____ Ev - 'ry

ooh. _____ Ev - 'ry

ooh. _____ Ev - 'ry

D.S.
(3rd time no repeat)

72

Dedicated to
The City High School Concert Choir, Iowa City, Iowa
Dr. Greg Grove, Director

Ezekiel Saw de Wheel

For SATB div. a cappella
Performance Time: Approx. 3:20

Traditional Spiritual
Arranged by MOSES HOGAN

*Pronounced throughout as E-ze-kul saw da wheel

Copyright © 2001 by HAL LEONARD CORPORATION
International Copyright Secured   All Rights Reserved

* Opt. octave higher throughout (if necessary)

wheel in a wheel in de mid-dle of de wheel way____ in de mid-dle of de air.

wheel in a wheel in de mid-dle of de wheel way____ in de mid-dle of de air.

wheel in a wheel in de mid-dle of de wheel way in de mid-dle of de air.

wheel in a wheel in de mid-dle of de wheel way____ in de mid-dle of de air.

Praise de Lawd! Praise de

Praise de Lawd! Praise de

I'm goin' jine* the heav'n-ly choir____ when dis worl' is set on fi-yer,

I'm goin' jine* the heav'n-ly choir____ when dis worl' is set on fi-yer,

* Pronounced *join*

* Start at slower tempo. *Gradual* accelerando to original tempo by m. 72 (as a wheel beginning to turn).

God's Gonna Set This World On Fire

For SATB a cappella
Performance Time: Approx. 3:20

Traditional Spiritual

Arranged by MOSES HOGAN
and EDWIN B. HOGAN

Copyright © 1995 by HAL LEONARD CORPORATION
International Copyright Secured All Rights Reserved

Commissioned by The North Carolina Music Educators Association Honor Choir, 2000
Frank Williams, Director

Good News, the Chariot's Comin'

For SATB a cappella

Performance Time: Approx. 2:40

Arranged by
MOSES HOGAN

Traditional Spiritual

Copyright © 2001 by HAL LEONARD CORPORATION
International Copyright Secured   All Rights Reserved

96

Commissioned by the musicians and music lovers of
Plymouth Congregational United Church of Christ, Des Moines, Iowa,
In Honor of Carol Stewart, Director of Music and Fine Arts (1967-1972, 1979-1993)

Great Day

For SATB a cappella and Solo
Performance Time: Approx. 2:30

Arranged by
MOSES HOGAN

Traditional Spiritual

Copyright © 1997 by HAL LEONARD CORPORATION
International Copyright Secured   All Rights Reserved

Dedicated to the memory of Jester Hairston

Hear My Prayer

For SATB a cappella
Performance Time: Approx. 2:25

Words and Music by
MOSES HOGAN

Copyright © 2001 by HAL LEONARD CORPORATION
International Copyright Secured   All Rights Reserved

* Close to "n" sound

Dedicated to Mr. Leo H. Davis, Jr. and the Mississippi Boulevard Christian Church
Sanctuary Choir of Memphis, TN, for their commitment to excellence in Church Music.

I Can Tell the World

For SATB div. a cappella
Performance Time: Approx. 3:00

Arranged by
MOSES HOGAN

Traditional Spiritual

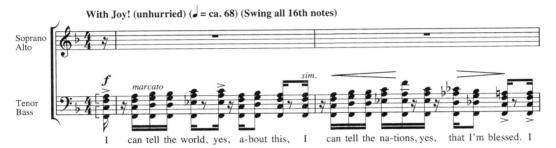

* close to "n"

Copyright © 1998 by HAL LEONARD CORPORATION
International Copyright Secured   All Rights Reserved

107

* close to "n"

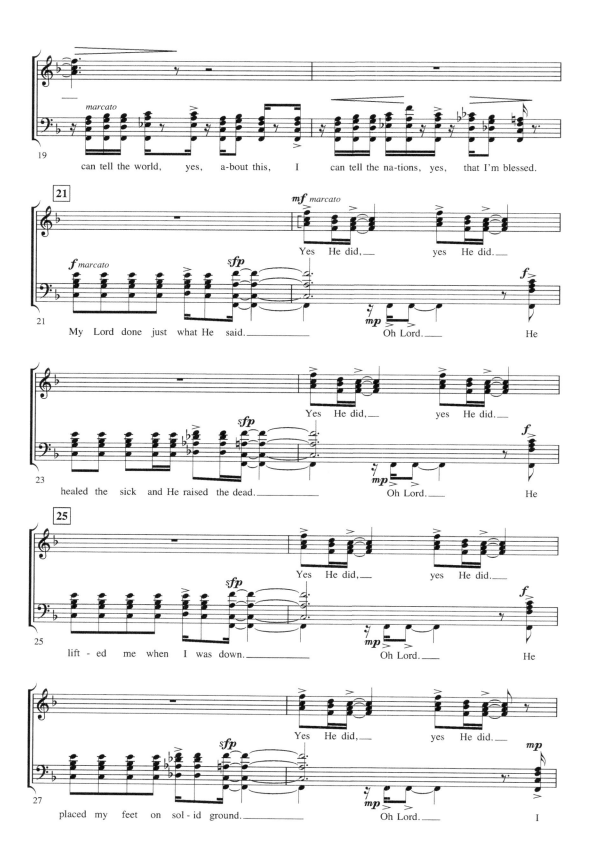

* close to "n"

* close to "n"

I Couldn't Hear Nobody Pray

For SATB div. a cappella and Solo

Performance Time: Approx. 3:00

**Arranged by
MOSES HOGAN**

Traditional Spiritual

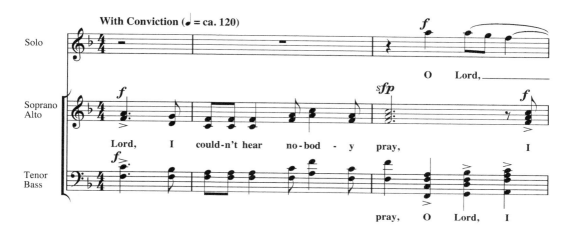

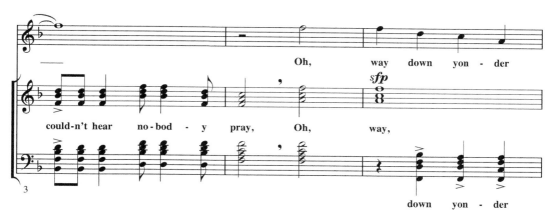

Copyright © 1999 by HAL LEONARD CORPORATION
International Copyright Secured   All Rights Reserved

I Got a Robe

For SATB a cappella and Solo

Performance Time: Approx. 2:10

Arranged by
MOSES HOGAN

Traditional Spiritual

Copyright © 1997 by HAL LEONARD CORPORATION
International Copyright Secured   All Rights Reserved

* Close to "nn" immediately on the word "heaven."

122

I GOT A ROBE – SATB

Dedicated to the Dillard University Choir
Mr. S. Carver Davenport, Director

I Know the Lord's Laid His Hands on Me

For SATB div. a cappella

Performance Time: Approx. 2:30

Traditional Spiritual

Arranged by
MOSES HOGAN

With Joy (♩ = *ca.* **50)**

Soprano
Alto

Tenor
Bass

Oh, I know the Lord, I know the Lord,

I know the Lord's laid His hands on me. Yes, I know the Lord,

I know the Lord, I know the Lord's laid His hands on me. Did

ev - er you see the light of day,

I know, Yes, I know that, my Lord's hands, He laid 'em.

Copyright © 1999 by HAL LEONARD CORPORATION
International Copyright Secured   All Rights Reserved

I know the Lord's— laid His hands on me. Oh, was-n't that a

I know, Yes, I know that,

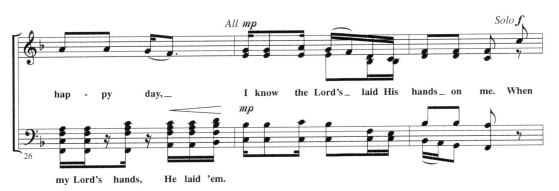

hap - py day,— I know the Lord's— laid His hands— on me. When

my Lord's hands, He laid 'em.

Je - sus washed my sins a - way?—

I know, Yes, I know that, my Lord's hands, He laid 'em.

I know the Lord's— laid His hands on me. Oh, I know the Lord,———

128

This Arrangement Dedicated to Dr. Samuel DuBois Cook

I Stood on the River of Jordan

For SATB a cappella
Performance Time: Approx. 4:30

Arranged by
MOSES HOGAN

Traditional Spiritual

Copyright © 1997 by HAL LEONARD CORPORATION
International Copyright Secured   All Rights Reserved

sis - ter you bet-tuh be read - y to see dat ship come sail - in' o - ber. O

broth - er you bet-tuh be read - y to see dat ship sail by. O

preach-er you bet-tuh be read - y to see dat ship come sail - in' o - ber. O

dea - con you bet-tuh be read - y to see dat ship sail by.

I Want Jesus to Walk with Me

For SATB a cappella
Performance Time: Approx. 3:30

Arranged by
MOSES HOGAN

Traditional Spiritual

Copyright © 1997 by HAL LEONARD CORPORATION
International Copyright Secured   All Rights Reserved

I Want to Be Ready

For SATB a cappella
Performance Time: Approx. 1:55

**Arranged by
MOSES HOGAN**

Traditional Spiritual

* **Swing 16th notes throughout**

Copyright © 2001 by HAL LEONARD CORPORATION
International Copyright Secured   All Rights Reserved

*close to "n" throughout.

*stay on vowel.

I Want To Thank You, Lord

For SATB a cappella and Soprano or Tenor Solo

Performance Time: Approx. 3:00

Arranged by
BENJAMIN HARLAN

Words and Music by
MOSES HOGAN

Copyright © 1995 by HAL LEONARD CORPORATION
International Copyright Secured All Rights Reserved

146

I'm Gonna Sing 'Til The Spirit Moves In My Heart

For SATB (divisi) a cappella

Performance Time: Approx. 2:10

Words and Music by
MOSES HOGAN

Copyright © 1995 by HAL LEONARD CORPORATION
International Copyright Secured   All Rights Reserved

* Pronounced "Je-su-sa."

152

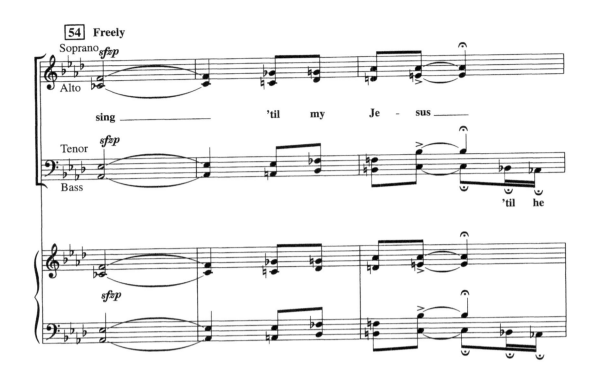

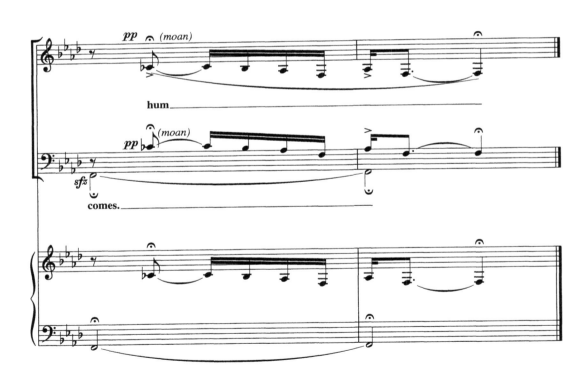

Jesus Lay Your Head in the Window

For SATB div. a cappella, Bass or Alto Solo and Flute

Performance Time: Approx. 4:25

Arranged by
MOSES HOGAN

Traditional Spiritual

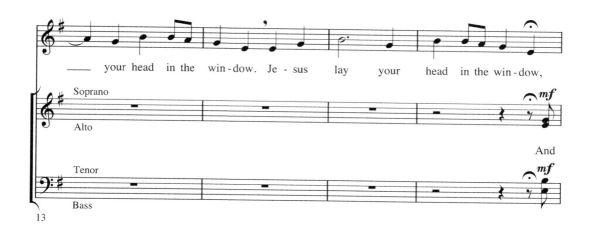

Copyright © 1998 by HAL LEONARD CORPORATION
International Copyright Secured   All Rights Reserved

162

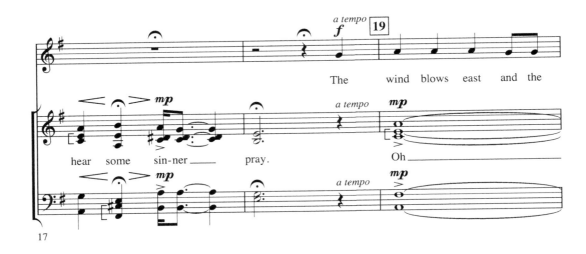

Commissioned by Dr. Walter J. Turnbull and
The Boys Choir of Harlem Inc.
For the 1998 Israel Tour

Little David, Play on Your Harp

For SATB a cappella
Performance Time: Approx. 3:30

Traditional Spiritual

Arranged by
MOSES HOGAN

Copyright © 1999 by HAL LEONARD CORPORATION
International Copyright Secured   All Rights Reserved

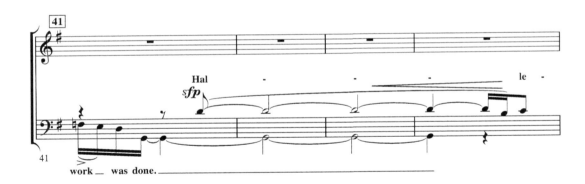

play on your harp, Hal - le - lu! Hal - le - lu-jah! Lit-tle Da - vid,

play on your harp, Hal - le - lu - jah.

Lit-tle Da - vid,

jah. *Hum.* Done told you once, done told you twice, There're sin-ners in hell for

Hum

shoot-in' dice.___ Done told you once, done told you twice, There're sin-ners in hell

Hum

for ___

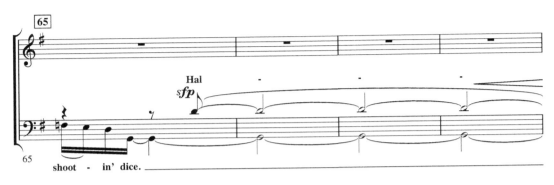

Lord, I Want to Be a Christian

For SATB a cappella

Performance Time: Approx. 3:40

Arranged by
MOSES HOGAN

Traditional Spiritual

Copyright © 1996 by HAL LEONARD CORPORATION
International Copyright Secured   All Rights Reserved

For Sonja Sepulveda and the Sumter High School Concert Choir
Premiered by SHS Concert Choir at the 1998 South Carolina ACDA

My Soul's Been Anchored in the Lord

For SATB div. a cappella

Performance Time: Approx. 2:45

Arranged by
MOSES HOGAN

Traditional Spiritual

* Pronounced "de"

Copyright © 1999 by HAL LEONARD CORPORATION
International Copyright Secured   All Rights Reserved

* Close to (n).

Dedicated to the Loyola University Concert Choir,
Meg Hulley, Director,
Loyola University, New Orleans

Oh Mary, Don't You Weep, Don't You Mourn

For SATB a cappella

Performance Time: Approx. 2:30

Arranged by MOSES HOGAN

Traditional Spiritual

Copyright © 2001 by HAL LEONARD CORPORATION
International Copyright Secured   All Rights Reserved

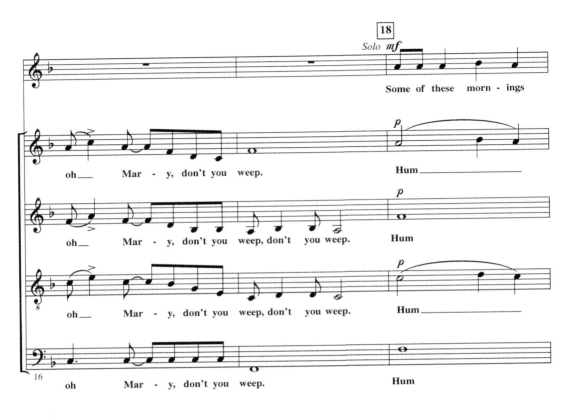

184

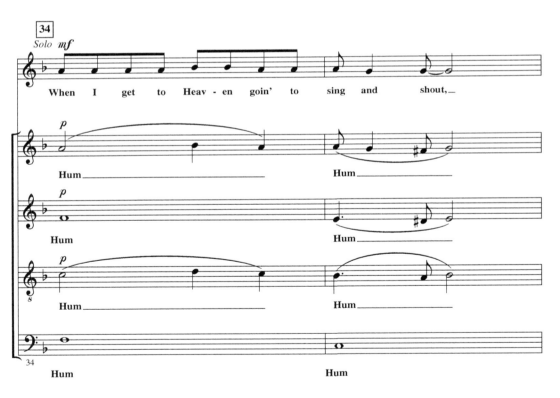

186

187

188

Dedicated to Albert McNeil
Celebrating the 35th Anniversary of The Albert McNeil Jubilee Singers

Ride the Chariot

For SATB div. a cappella
Performance Time: Approx. 2:30

Arranged by
MOSES HOGAN

African-American Spiritual

*observe phrase markings

Copyright © 2001 by HAL LEONARD CORPORATION
International Copyright Secured   All Rights Reserved

For the Bear River and Box Elder High School Choirs
Garland and Brigham City, Utah
Brian Peterson and Claudia Bigler, Directors

Standing in the Need of Prayer

For SATB a cappella
Performance Time: Approx. 2:30

Traditional Spiritual

**Arranged by
MOSES HOGAN**

Copyright © 1999 by HAL LEONARD CORPORATION
International Copyright Secured   All Rights Reserved

196

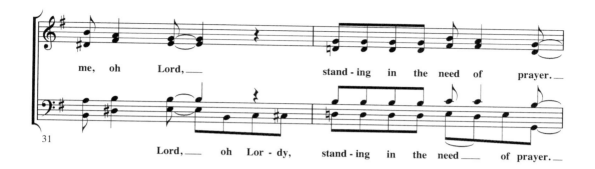

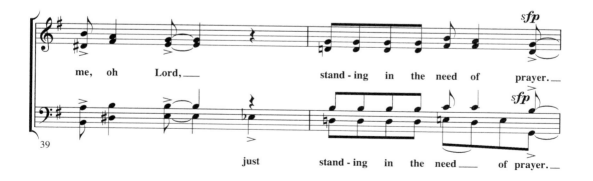

198

Steal Away

For SATB a cappella
Performance Time: Approx. 5:40

**Arranged by
MOSES HOGAN**

Traditional Spiritual

Copyright © 1999 by HAL LEONARD CORPORATION
International Copyright Secured   All Rights Reserved

Dedicated to Barbara Hendricks

There Is a Balm in Gilead

For SATB div. a cappella and Solo
Performance Time: Approx. 3:30

Arranged by
MOSES HOGAN

Traditional Spiritual

Copyright © 1998 by HAL LEONARD CORPORATION
International Copyright Secured   All Rights Reserved

206

Dedicated to the St. Olaf Choir
Dr. Anton Armstrong, Conductor

This Little Light of Mine

For SATB div. a cappella

Performance Time: Approx. 3:40

Traditional Spiritual
Arranged by MOSES HOGAN

Copyright © 2002 by HAL LEONARD CORPORATION
International Copyright Secured   All Rights Reserved

208

210

Close to an "n" sound (not too quickly)

* Close to an "n" sound (not too quickly)

Wade in the Water

For SATB a cappella and Solo

Performance Time: Approx. 3:30

Arranged by
MOSES HOGAN

Traditional Spiritual

* *Choir should sing "water" with a voiced "t." Soloist should sing "wa-der" throughout.*

Copyright © 1997 by HAL LEONARD CORPORATION
International Copyright Secured   All Rights Reserved

220

Commissioned by The Liberty Senior High School Concert Choir, Liberty, Missouri, Debra Burnett, Director

Walk Together, Children

For SATB div. a cappella
Performance Time: Approx. 3:05

**Arranged by
MOSES HOGAN**

Traditional Spiritual

Note: "don't you" should be sung "don'cha" and "tire" should
be sung "ti-yer" (as written) unless held as one syllable.

Copyright © 2001 by HAL LEONARD CORPORATION
International Copyright Secured   All Rights Reserved

Dedicated to The Calvin College Alumni Choir
Pearl Shangkuan, Conductor

We Shall Walk Through the Valley in Peace

For SATB div. a cappella
Performance Time: Approx. 4:20

Arranged by
MOSES HOGAN

African-American Spiritual

Copyright © 2001 by HAL LEONARD CORPORATION
International Copyright Secured   All Rights Reserved

230

232

Published Works by Moses Hogan
Hal Leonard Corporation

SATB Unaccompanied Works

Abide With Me, 08703227
Ain't That Good News, 08740662
Battle of Jericho, The, 08703139
Cert'nly Lawd, 08743356
De Blin' Man Stood on de Road an' Cried, 08703261
Didn't My Lord Deliver Daniel, 08703209
Do Lord, Remember Me, 08703326
Down by the Riverside, 08703201
Elijah Rock, 08705532
Ev'ry Time I Feel the Spirit, 08740285
Ezekiel Saw de Wheel, 08703327
Give Me Jesus, 08703202
Glory, Glory, Glory to the Newborn King, 08742097
God's Gonna Set This World on Fire, 08740286
Good News, The Chariot's Comin', 08703312
Great Day, 08741181
Hear My Prayer, 08703308
Hold On, 08703351
I Can Tell the World, 08703198
I Couldn't Hear Nobody Pray, 08703239
I Got a Home in a dat Rock, 08703228
I Got a Robe, 08741179
I Know the Lord's Laid His Hands on Me, 08703232
I Stood on the River of Jordan, 08741178
I Want Jesus to Walk with Me, 08740785
I Want To Be Ready, 08703310
I Want To Thank You, Lord, 08740200
I'm Gonna Sing 'til the Spirit Moves in My Heart, 08740284
Jesus Lay Your Head in the Window, 08703199
Lift Every Voice for Freedom, 08711353
Little David, Play on Your Harp, 08703229
Lord, I Want To Be a Christian, 08703140
Mister Banjo, 08740600
My Soul's Been Anchored in the Lord, 08703235
No Hidin' Place, 08703328
Oh Mary, Don't You Weep, Don't You Mourn, 08703329
Old Time Religion, 08740181
Ride the Chariot, 08703309
A Spiritual Reflection, 08703315
Stand By Me, 08743328
Standing in the Need of Prayer, 08703230
Steal Away, 08703203
Surely He Died on Calvary, 08703331
There Is a Balm in Gilead, 08703200
This Little Light of Mine, 08743115
Wade in the Water, 08741180
Walk Together, Children, 08703332